Nesting

CO-PARENTING TO CONTINUE THE NUCLEAR FAMILY AFTER DIVORCE

● ● ●

Lucenda Jacobs

ISBN-13: 9780999151525
ISBN-10: 0999151525
The Sunlit Company, Bellaire, Texas

Nesting

To my children

Contents

Preface

● ● ●

WHEN I WAS RESEARCHING HOW to structure co-parenting with my ex-husband, I found few resources on the parenting arrangement called "bird's nest" co-parenting or "nesting." I found no firsthand accounts. This book, in which I provide a detailed description of my experience with nesting, is meant to alleviate that frustration for others. The story I tell is about how my family continues to live as a nuclear family now that my children's father and I are divorced. My ex-husband and I still parent together. We are both still in our children's lives completely, and we live in harmony. This is a story about finding a sunlit path to parenting after divorce, through nesting.

Acknowledgments

● ● ●

MY HEARTFELT THANKS TO MY friends for their encouragement and support through all things having to do with this book.

The Flood

● ● ●

Everybody has a plan until they
get punched in the mouth

MIKE TYSON

"Lucy." My husband called my name softly, as he often did when he needed to convey important information. "Water is coming into the house."

I felt a twinge of irritation. I knew that he was asking me to wake up at two in the morning to take charge of the problem, likely a leak around a window or maybe even a leak in the roof. It would be up to me, yet again, to solve the problem with the house I had named Casa della Luna. Even after seven years of me solving problems or giving him directions on what needed to be done, I still maintained the childish fantasy that one day, he would handle things. He would see a problem, and without even letting me know about it, he would take care of it.

I ignored him. I also ignored the blaring sound of an emergency broadcast coming from the television in the living room. As usual, he had fallen asleep on the couch watching it. The flash-flood warning had been sounding periodically since before I went to bed that night. "I guess Harris County wants me to fix that problem too," I thought.

I relaxed and let the sound of the bittersweet rain lull me back to sleep. I dreamed of my husband suddenly becoming a competent handyman.

About an hour later, I was awakened again, this time by the sound of one of my dogs lapping up water. That was curious. Why would King be drinking water in my bedroom?

I had been mentally checked out of my marriage until nature got my attention early that Memorial Day morning. My husband and I had been unhappily staying in our marriage, because I thought it was the noble thing to do. I thought it was best for our children. I wanted our children to have a home where they had access to both parents every day. I wanted them to grow up with traditions built on family and celebrations and holidays. I wanted them to live in a neighborhood where they had friends and a sense of community. Having a house that anchored us together in that community was also a plus. All these ideas I tied to being married to their father.

Once I realized that Brays Bayou was now flowing through my house, I had no choice but to respond. I grew up in Houston, so this wasn't my first rodeo with fast-rising water. My husband and kids were already at it, with towels, mops, bowls, buckets—anything they could think of that might hold back the water that was rising in our home. Even the dogs seemed to be doing their part by lapping up as much water as they could. It at first had escaped me, the fact that my husband had taken charge after I had ignored his request for my attention earlier. There was a lesson in that fact for both of us that we would only recognize once we separated. In the meantime, I joined them in the task at hand and we worked together. Everyone knew what the goal was: stop more water from coming into the house. We were in a flurry of activity.

We worked like beavers, so focused on our goal of saving our house and all that was in it that we neglected to consider a basic fact: water conducts electricity. We were glad that the electricity was still flowing through the wiring in the house. It was 3:00 a.m., and without it we would not be able to see what we were doing. We were working to make our house, and all that it represented, do its job. Its job was to keep us safe and dry, warm in the winter, and cool in the summer. We would not give up our house to the water we were standing in.

Seven years earlier, the first summer we spent in Casa della Luna, Hurricane Ike hit our spot on the Gulf Coast. Most people in the city were without power for days, if not weeks, after that storm blew through. Our house didn't flood in that event. Nor did our house lose power at any point during or after the storm. Ours was only one of a few houses in the neighborhood that had electricity for that posthurricane period for which emergency supplies are kept. Friends, family, and neighbors used our house as a brief refuge in the aftermath of Ike. Our house offered relief during that time of trouble, even if it was just for those without electricity in their houses to charge a cell phone or to get a good night's sleep in air conditioning. We liked that about this house. The fact that others could come to our home and feel like they had found a beacon of light made us believe that our house had its own purpose, almost a life of its own. This added to its mystique for us, for it was easy to fantasize that this was a special, almost magical place. We felt it was more than just a house.

Now, as we worked, it felt like the house was taking care of us again, by keeping the lights on and the air conditioning working. But it couldn't, really; it was only a house. The comfort we felt in this inanimate object was generated by our minds and our experiences. We didn't think that our fantasy about this house could be dangerous to our well-being. The water rose to a point above the power outlets, and I now credit our survival of that flood as partially due to the updated electrical panel that we had installed in the fifty-year-old house when we moved in. Still in comfort, we continued to try to stop the water from coming in. Then, in a moment of clarity, we realized that we could not stop the water from coming in. It didn't feel like a failure, just a realization.

We switched gears. We stopped trying to save the house and focused on trying to save what was in it. We were still excited from the shock of what was happening, and adrenaline was flowing. We moved things out of the way of the water, starting with what we thought was most important. I didn't have to worry about photos or keepsakes, as I kept those things either on the wall or on a high shelf—I had had a little foresight. So I went to what I thought was practical. I started picking up all the shoes off the floor. While I was doing that, I remembered a bottom drawer in the hallway where I kept some bedding, which at the time I thought was more important than shoes. So I left the shoes and went to move the bedding.

We were trying to hold on to what had been our reality, our belief in how things were supposed to be. But the bayou had a new reality it would share with us, and once we accepted it, the stress of the struggle melted away. Everything was put into perspective. All we could do was to seek higher ground; water seeks its own level and will find it, even if it has to go through your living room.

Trying to maintain a marriage that had run its course was like trying to keep the water of Brays Bayou out of that house. The house was directly in the middle of the bayou's newly determined path. My marriage was like that house, Casa della Luna, which is

Italian for "House of the Moon." And like a house on the moon would be, it had become a cold, lifeless place, even though my husband and I were still very much alive and in search of the freedom to be ourselves that we couldn't find with each other. We were stranded in a dark and dreary place, which may have from a distance looked beautifully mysterious and romantic.

There was no stopping the movement that had so rudely entered our house uninvited early that morning. The rising had become a flow, slow and deliberate like the bayou it was. There was an instant sense of freedom when we all stopped fighting the flowing water. We had no choice but to let it run its course. We accepted that this water, this flood, would occupy every inch of space in Casa della Luna. Once we stopped focusing on something we couldn't change, my husband and I turned our focus to what was most important to us: our children.

We knew it was time to leave. Fortunately, we had introduced ourselves to our new neighbors a few months earlier with cookies that my daughter had made and a birdhouse that my son had built. The neighbors had a newer house, and its living space was at least six feet higher than ours. They gave us shelter until the sun came up and we could assess the damage. It was complete. The rescue effort was now a recovery effort.

We started doing what we knew had to be done. We removed everything that the bayou had touched on its way through our house. We started to remove from the house all those things that were no longer of use to us and put them on the curb. So much had become refuse—things without purpose—in a matter of hours.

One of my closest friends came by a day or so after the flood to assess the damage. He described the scene on our street as a disaster zone. He recognized it for what it was at that moment. He's the one who helped me to see the house for what it really was, just "sticks and bricks," as he said. Exactly, it was just sticks and bricks, and it had always been that. A small shift in perspective made all the difference. Before he had pointed that out, it was still Casa della Luna in my mind, and it was suffering the aftereffects of a disaster. The president had even declared it so, and it definitely felt that way for a while. But the glimpse of reality that my friend gave me helped me start to look for a new path through the rubble. I could start with clearer vision and be more objective about it.

When one of my sisters came by to help, she also shed some light on the situation. She did so by giving me an even better perspective. She was standing with me in my water-soaked kitchen as I was taking one item at a time out of the bottom cabinets. I did so very carefully. I opened each cabinet door very slowly of course, in case the bayou had left any of its cold-blooded inhabitants trapped inside. My sister asked me what I was doing. I told her I had to go through all those things to see what could be saved. Then I told her how I would need to clean whatever could be saved and pack it away. I told her this would take days, even weeks. I told her indignantly that that's what you do after a flood. I expected her sympathy and offers of help with the daunting task, but instead I got what sisters are good for: a critique, straight with no chaser. She told me that I was delusional and that I needed to take everything in the kitchen out to the curb, or better yet, hire someone else to do it. She told me to just walk away, start over, and realize that my efforts were not worth it. I told her about all the things in that kitchen that took me years to accumulate and how attached I was to some of them. She said, "OK, suit yourself." Then I thought about it, and there was relief in just the thought alone. I stopped the recovery-of-things effort immediately. Soon, what at first had seemed like disaster began to feel like a cleansing, as I saw that we were left with not so much an empty house as a clean slate. We were all still dazed, but we were starting to figure out that the flood had simply changed our course.

The flood taught us that security is an illusion. Disasters happen. Clean up, and move on. If you have flood insurance, great; use it.

However, there's no such thing as marriage insurance. Expect that sometimes the unexpected will come and change how you see things. When you find yourself in a situation where you need to seek higher ground, be flexible. Understand the terrain. Move forward. Then find a better place to settle and continue your journey.

For a few months after the flood, we lived like refugees. It was during this time that my husband and I decided to divorce. It would take a year for us to reconstruct our settled living situation. But when we did, it was much better. The way we live now supports continued growth for everyone, and it considers all our needs. We are still working together toward a common goal, but now we do it with the freedom of a lighter load. Gone is the burden of trying to maintain a house in which frustration, irritation, annoyance, and sometimes anger created tension between two people who no longer wanted to be married.

My children still reap the rewards of growing up in a nuclear family. They live in a house in a neighborhood that gives them a sense of community. My ex-husband and I both commit our financial resources to maintaining a home that supports them and ourselves in whatever ways we need. He and I maintain, separately, the family and holiday traditions that we value for our children. We socialize with friends and family in much the same ways as we did before we divorced: I with the children with my friends and family, and he with the children with his friends and family. We both communicate openly and spontaneously with our children, and we regularly give them affection and emotional support.

Even though our marriage ended, the nuclear family that my ex-husband and I created remains. We transitioned our family into a nesting living situation that allows us to maintain a two-parent household that exists for the primary benefit of our children. It is the best option for us, and I want to share our story. I believe that nesting is a new American institution that has expanded the options for the structure of the nuclear family.

CHAPTER 1

Trinity

● ● ●

You have to love your children unselfishly.
That's hard. But it's the only way.

BARBARA BUSH

MY CHILDREN LOVE THEIR FATHER. I guess it's true, blood is thicker than water. I have found a new way to relate to him. I have always liked that my children have a true affection for the man I chose as their dad. I often jokingly tell people that my children like their father more than they like me. He guards their affection like the precious jewel it is. It comes first for him. I appreciate and respect that quality about him. It gives me a sense of peace to know that there is someone else in my children's lives who will be there for them no matter what. My ex-husband and I both will be there for them to the level of rearranging our lives to better suit their needs.

My children have affection for me also, but I am not as careful with it as their father is. I know that whether they like me at any one time will take a subordinate position to my doing what is best for them. Homework, Internet, responsibility, respect, and food can all be topics of contention more with me than with their father. Those things, reflecting some of the many ways that my ex-husband and I differ in our parenting styles, are just part of how I plan to influence them now.

My path from love to something close to indifference about my marriage and my husband was just one of the many that people take. But where my path branches off is in how I decided I wanted to parent our children after our divorce. I wanted to divorce my husband, but I wanted to maintain our nuclear family.

A casual conversation I had with an aunt who was married to a European first made me believe it was possible to maintain a nuclear family after divorce. My aunt was relating how differently family and children are sometimes handled in Europe compared to the United States. Her husband's granddaughter was the subject of a custody dispute. The judge presiding over the case told her parents that they would have to take care of her in the home she grew up in until she was twenty-five.

Now for how true and accurate this story is, I cannot be held accountable. I could be remembering it wrong, or my aunt could have told it wrong. All I know is that whatever the story was, it piqued my curiosity and opened a thought process in my mind. I began to investigate ways that children could remain in the family home after divorce. I had heard of this in the context of Hollywood couples or the super-rich, whose kids were basically raised by nannies, and they, the parents, just visited occasionally. But then I read something about nesting. It was a form of parenting that real people did. I didn't know anyone who did it, but I knew it was something I wanted to do.

I didn't find much literature on the subject and no firsthand accounts at all. But I was undeterred. I knew that this living and parenting arrangement would make my family life better.

I didn't decide to divorce my children's father when I was angry at him. He probably would have liked that. At one point, before I became more self-aware and less focused on him, he would have felt relieved by my asking him to leave the family home. He would have seen himself finally having the freedom he had so hoped for in our marriage. When I was angry at him, life at Casa della Luna was not pleasant for anyone, especially not for him. When I felt betrayed by him, those underlying currents of frustration, irritation, and disappointment that had been part of our marriage for years were joined by angst and dismay. And I was not one to suffer in silence. I needed to be heard, and if I didn't feel that I was being heard, I protested.

I needed relief from my angst and dismay, and I labored for a while under the false assumption that he could be cajoled into giving me that relief. I kept searching for signs that he understood how I felt. I kept asking him to relieve me of this incongruent understanding of our relationship that I was forced to try to make sense of. He would not or could not. The unfortunate side effect of this obsession I had with trying to get him to do something he didn't want to do was my laser-like focus on him. Everything else took a back seat, including my children.

It was only after burning through the heat of my self-righteous indignation over his failure to be accountable for my happiness that I realized that I was asking him for something he didn't have. He didn't have the ability or desire to be what I wanted him to be. It turned out that he wasn't willing to play a supporting role in my story anymore. He felt that he had never gotten it right anyway, and it no longer appealed to him. I understood, and I empathized with him. The thought of trying to get a man whom I wanted as a partner to do something he didn't want to do was unpleasant for me. I wanted to share my life with someone who had his own story, one I could admire and make guest appearances in occasionally. Hopefully, that partner would want to do the same for me.

That was it. That was the realization that made me unable to envision a future with my children's father as my husband or lover. I no longer wanted him as a partner. I knew I didn't want to share a bedroom with him anymore. I no longer could reserve those two roles, husband and lover, for him. The father role, however, the third pillar in what I consider the holy trinity of family, was not mine to discard. In fact, I wanted to preserve it, for me and my children.

I had, years before, forsaken the lover in the man I was married to. The husband role, however, was still something I had envisioned for him right up until the flood. It was a diminished vision, but I still had expectations. I was led to believe, through popular media and pseudo social-scientific pronouncements on the Internet, that lots of marriages continue without the lover role. It didn't sound like something I would have ever volunteered for, but if circumstances required it, I was willing to go with it.

He didn't seem to notice. The fact that we had come to some sort of equilibrium about our relationship seemed to be enough for him. He may have checked out long ago. This was the state of our marriage. We continued living with each other and the children as a nuclear family. That was the plan. As long as we didn't dig too deep and expect too much, it would be OK. I wanted to maintain our family structure for our children. To me, the house that we lived in, Casa della Luna, was as vital to our nuclear family as our marriage. Everything I thought about raising children revolved around a marriage and a house. I couldn't see things differently. I had white-picket-fence syndrome.

The children had friends down that street whom they used to play with before they discovered computer games and the Internet. They didn't go to the neighborhood elementary school, so most of their friends didn't live in our neighborhood. But Casa della Luna was where many of the milestones in their lives happened. When we first moved into that house, my son couldn't reach the light switch in the kitchen. He would get a long wooden spoon out of a drawer that he could reach, and he used it to push up the light switch to turn on the lights. They learned to ride their bikes on our street. We planted a lemon tree in the backyard and got an abundance of lemons two years later. It was where I hoped they would bring their children for Thanksgiving. I still imagined it being the family home, in both the present and the future. However, I hadn't quite squared that vision of our family's future with the reality that I couldn't imagine a happy personal future with their father. But never mind that—I had to maintain. So I maintained.

The only options I could see were to maintain, to the best of my ability, a home where we all lived together as a family, or I would break my children's hearts by diminishing the role of their father in their lives. I couldn't do either. As their mother, I believe one of my obligations to them is to provide a foundation from which they can grow into their own stories with as little interference from my shortcomings as possible. One of my shortcomings was that I was no longer able to put the desire to not be married to their father behind their need for him in their lives. I could not stay married to their father.

However, I had made my children the primary beneficiaries of this family that I had created with their father. The combined effort that he and I undertook created a home where we could help our hopes and dreams for our children blossom. When we did that, we wholeheartedly believed that the family we were creating was for our benefit as well. It was our shared project, a manifestation of our love for each other. Our family would be the airstrip from which we would all take off and fly. However, the love and affection we wanted to give our children along with the guidance and direction they needed were being undermined by our crumbling marriage story. We could not find a way to rewrite it so that it worked.

Even with our faults, all the elements to make our nuclear family a success were in place. We had dinner together almost every evening. We celebrated holidays and birthdays, created traditions, entertained one another, and went on vacations. All the makings of a nuclear family, which would just about guarantee my kids a healthy start to building their own lives as adults, were there. But other things were also present in their lives; they were the underlying currents that often distracted my husband and me and sometimes kept us from being the parents we wanted to be. And those currents were growing.

We were no longer lovers, but he was still my husband and my children's father. The husband role still carried a lot of weight for both of us. I still had expectations, and he still resented them. I had never really handed the husband role over to him completely. I had an image of what I wanted in a husband. Included in that image was what I thought was plenty of room for him to be himself. He, on the other hand, expected me to let him be the husband he chose to be without exception. We could never come to an agreement on who got to define the husband role. I also had an image of what kind of father I hoped he would be, and fortunately, I had a lot more flexibility in my expectations for that role. But ultimately, I recognized that the father role belonged to my husband and our children. I was merely a trustee with a fiduciary duty, I felt, to handle it strictly from the position of what was best for my children. They were the beneficiaries, and until they were old enough to take it over completely, I had to preserve it as best I could, which for the most part meant staying out of the way of their relationship with their father. I understood that while they are still children, the mother and father roles are so intertwined that if one suffers, they both suffer. That's why I tried to maintain what was left of the trinity: husband and father. But I put too much emphasis on the husband role. I was constantly examining it because we were always there together, and when we were together, those undercurrents rose up. The husband role as interpreted by the father of my children didn't work for me. But I still couldn't face letting it go, because I didn't realize that it wasn't essential to having a nuclear family.

When my ex-husband and I first met, I thought he had it all. I quickly saw in him a husband, father, and lover—not necessarily in that order. I saw what I wanted to see. In my eyes, he fit the bill as all three, or at least as my versions of all three. He would be the pillar on which I built my family. He would hold us all up, me and my children. He seemed capable.

I am tempted to include a glimpse of his version of our story here also, but I know it's not possible. I would only be telling my view of what I think he would say. But even at the beginning of our story, I knew there were undercurrents going against us—unmet needs and different desires and expectations—but I could accept that. I wasn't looking for a perfect family, just one that would be successful. For me, a successful family meant having people who are intimately close and would always be included in one another's lives, be interested in one another's details, and would be mutually affirming and supportive. We would share the good and the bad. We would all be individuals whose stories overlapped—my story, his story, our kids' stories. Stories would come together and sometimes collide in the place called family.

My husband's and my stories definitely collided; we couldn't get them to come together in a harmonious way. We were on different wavelengths. When I needed more emotional intimacy, he needed space. When he needed reassurance, I was far away in my own galaxy. We both felt too distant and too misunderstood to understand, much less meet, each other's needs. Our expressions of need were like signals sent out by SETI that, it was hoped, would one day be picked up and understood. But we couldn't reach each other. We were light-years apart. The great expanse between us became an entanglement of unfilled needs, resentment, and perpetual frustrations. It was painful for both of us.

Although it wasn't visible to the naked eye, the thing between us gave off evidence of its existence. It had begun to take up all the space in the family home. It was extinguishing the hearth, that part of the home that gives it life. The energy from it was sapping the energy and liveliness from our home—so much so that the kids' stories, even though they continued, incorporated some of the shrapnel of the discord between my husband and me. Their stories had to be pushed down and conformed to ours. But we still maintained our marriage, because the nuclear family was still the best option in our minds.

My marriage was always about my husband and me. The children were just along for the ride. The same is true about our divorce. It was about us not being right for each other. We divorced because we stopped pretending that something would be different. We finally accepted that we would not learn some totally new way of relating to each other or have an epiphany and suddenly "get" each other so we could meet each other's needs or wants. We were not going to fundamentally change. We knew that. To be clear, if we hadn't had children, we probably would have divorced sooner. But we do have children, so we stayed married longer than we should have. We couldn't figure out how to successfully parent outside of a marriage. We had no examples that we wanted to follow.

CHAPTER 2

A Bayou Runs through It

● ● ●

The bond that links your true family is not one of
blood, but of respect and joy in each other's life.

RICHARD BACH

MY EXPERIENCE HAS TAUGHT ME that a nuclear family is more than
just the sum of its parts. There are parts of it that are visible to
all, parts that can only be seen by the members of that family,
and other parts that can't be seen at all, but only felt. And then,
some parts can only be known in hindsight. How all these parts
come together is what makes a nuclear family. And each family
member has a different view and experience of these parts. There
are undertones and currents, phases and tensions, all able to have
negative or positive effects on members of the family.

The image of the nuclear family that I grew up with was that
of a mother, a father, and their children all living together in a
house in the suburbs. That's what I saw on TV and around me in
my neighborhood on the southeast side of Houston. I grew up in
the seventies, and from what I now understand from popular culture, that was a tumultuous time for families compared to earlier

decades. Even so, the traditional nuclear-family model still represented the ideal for me.

I grew up in a working-class neighborhood with many types of families. There were single-parent households and maybe some families headed by grandparents, but for the most part, I saw families with married parents raising their children together.

I also knew that a lot went on in those families that would not be seen as healthy by today's standards. Corporal punishment was the rule. I had friends who often didn't want to go home because they feared a brutal punishment for some infraction. Almost everyone I knew accepted beatings as normal. I do remember one or two kids in my neighborhood who never got a "whooping," as we called it. They were an oddity. Sometimes, children were left home alone at a much younger age than is allowed by law today. I could go on, but it's not necessary for my story.

My parents divorced before I entered elementary school, and my mother remarried as soon as she could. I rarely saw my father or spoke to him after my parents' divorce. He lived in another state, and I only remember visiting him once in the summer when I was in elementary school.

My mother made it clear that her remarrying had nothing to do with providing a certain type of home life for her children. She remarried only to quell her fear of her parents' disapproval of her being single and pregnant again. How she was viewed by her family of origin was infinitely more important to her than the life her children had to live. She made sure that I knew that I was not a child that she wanted; I just happened to be there. I was a burden that she carried resentfully. Once, when I was nine or ten, I went to her for support after an altercation with one of my cousins. She offered me no comfort, only this advice: "You had better get used to being mistreated because you will have a hard life, because you're ugly." I was stunned, and even at that age, I understood that she was not capable of comforting me. Her experiences made her so myopic that the beauty of her own child escaped her. This made me very deliberate in my procreation and family building. I didn't have my first child until I was thirty-eight years old. It wasn't because I didn't have the opportunity before that age. In fact, at thirty-eight I was in my second marriage. My first marriage had ended without children. I thought my first husband would make a great father, but after a few years of marriage, I knew I wouldn't be happy with him as a husband. I guess I was paying closer attention the first time. I wanted to make sure I didn't pass on to my children that feeling of being an inconvenient burden to be suffered through. I did my best to make sure my children knew they were wanted and loved by both their parents.

My understanding was that a family should provide a place of beginnings from which children can be grounded, from which the trajectory of their lives can be set in a direction of positivity or negativity. I wanted to set my children's trajectory in a positive direction. Of course, I knew that nothing was guaranteed. There isn't always a positive correlation between the quality of children's upbringings and the quality of their adult lives. Ultimately, people create their own experiences and stories. But I would do my best to help their stories start out in love, joy, and peace.

My ex-husband had a different upbringing. He grew up in the Bronx with his mother, father, and younger brother. His father was a World War II veteran who went to college at night so that he could provide a better life for his family. He was unnecessarily harsh with his family, and my ex-husband said that he never felt safe around his father.

His mother was a housewife. She was the only child of German immigrants. In my ex-husband's eyes, she played a passive role. It seems that no one, neither her children nor her husband or her parents, expected much of her. She didn't let anyone down.

My ex-husband's parents eventually divorced, but it was after he had already left home. His memories of his nuclear family were tarnished by the way his father treated his mother. His father didn't seem to like her very much and sometimes beat her. This was during the fifties and sixties, so it was not unheard of. I can't say what effect my ex-husband's upbringing had on him, but I'm sure it had an effect, as it would have for most of us.

Neither my husband nor I wanted our broken and sometimes nonsensical early life stories to make potholes in the runway we were building for our children. Our desire to prevent the damaged parts of our lives from affecting our children's lives was not enough. We were incapable of stepping outside the roles of needy children enough to make our marriage story different. Somewhere in the recesses of our closed and unconscious minds, we had decided not to make it better. We were no longer interested in the roles that had first brought us together, husband and wife and lovers. But we were still together, holding this family format together for our children.

Even a home where all the members of the nuclear family live 100 percent of the time can still be broken or dysfunctional. My husband and I both knew that firsthand. We never strove for our family to be completely free of conflict; we just wanted one where we could be together and share in the benefits of that togetherness. I knew that no family was perfect, and there would be trials and tests. I wouldn't want a family without any difficulty anyway. How could I truly appreciate the good times completely if I never had some not-so-great times to compare them with?

I also knew—still know—that many people still believe that you stay married no matter what, for better or for worse. I understand that principle, but I never found a compelling enough reason to buy into it. On a micro, individual level, it doesn't make sense to me. I understand the religious and social arguments for not divorcing. There can be beauty in suffering and sacrifice. But there can also be beauty in letting go of the struggle.

My husband and I both had a heart for the sanctity of our children's home life. It was the reason we did a lot of the things we did. But our heads and hearts were locked in ego-driven conflict that made our home less than a sanctuary for our children. The struggle for our marriage wasn't worth it. There were four lives at stake in this struggle. We could have chosen to continue the struggle, in hopes that one day the veil would be lifted from our eyes, and we would finally be able to see each other we way we wanted to be seen. But after fifteen years, I believe we had gotten to the essence of our issue: we were not a good match. Both of us would have to give up the hope of ever having much of what we desired in a partner, and that would be nothing less than tragic.

My reluctance to divorce was partly based on my belief that marriage was essential to the nuclear-family structure. A man and a woman were legally bound to give their full support and attention to the family they had created and vowed to maintain. I had created this family with my husband, and I would see it through, I thought. Unfortunately, although I was reluctant to divorce, I was not reluctant to let go of the animosity that had built up between us. I was in an almost constant state of frustration, irritation, aggravation, or upset. I knew that the marriage was not meant to continue. But under the assumption that staying married was what was best for my children, we let our negative undercurrents run rampant beneath the surface. The relationship between us was reduced to resentful roommates—the type that get assigned in the first year of college, quickly realize they have nothing in common, and just try to stay out of each other's way. The kids knew there was trouble; there was no hiding it.

I felt almost the same way about a house's role in a nuclear family as I did about a marriage, but the flood cleared that myth up for me quickly. A house is just sticks and bricks filled with stuff, as my good friend had told me. Mine had almost become an obstacle in my quest for a peaceful and happy nuclear family. It was the site and subject of many marital arguments. My ex-husband grew up in an apartment and never liked doing home maintenance. He felt that spending his Saturday doing yard work or repairs was a waste. I, on the other hand, spent lots of time at the home-improvements store. I was always working on some home project. It's in my nature, and I like being close to home. With my fondness for Casa della Luna, I would have thought that its destruction in a flood would have been emotionally hard for me. But it wasn't. There was something almost cathartic about the way it was swept out of my life.

After the flood, we had to move three times before we finally settled into our nest. There were so many things that had to be taken care of, and I had to do it all. But this time, I did not put up a fuss about it. I knew it would be that way: I would be in almost continuous motion and my husband, seemingly to counter my motion, would try to do as little as possible.

As soon as the water receded from the house, I initiated all movement toward getting our family taken care of. I understood my husband well enough by this point to know that he was slower to react in most situations than I was. He also had no problem with having me make decisions. In fact, he preferred it. This was an unfortunate mismatch for us. His passiveness with tasks often left me feeling overwhelmed and unsupported. I was resentful that he allowed himself to coast along while I handled things. I wanted to be able to do that too. But he somehow always beat me to the passenger side of our marital vehicle. I felt that he forced me into the driver's seat. He often said, "I don't know what to do," when it came to most things domestic. So I had to become the problem solver, facing the world and making things happen. This was a profound disappointment to me. It went against my nature. I needed to have a full partner in a husband. That had always been a complaint of mine, and one of the things he felt he could never live up to: taking care of me the way I wanted him to.

I once tried to draw an analogy to demonstrate how I hoped our marriage would work. He was a musician, so he understood what it meant to work in concert with another musician, and how both musicians needed to learn the ways of the other, to almost instinctively understand their movements and rhythm and be able to read when they were about to make a change. He knew how both musicians needed to support each other, knowing when to lead and when to follow. Good musicians strove to work together so they could react almost from instinct. He understood how the give-and-take helped music flow and allowed for spontaneous new expressions from both players because they were in it together, and each supported what the other was doing. If one started to riff, the other naturally fell back in a supportive mode. Then the other would take the lead and let the first one ride along.

Of course, my husband took that whole diatribe as another long belittling of him, which of course it was. It was me telling him again how inadequate he was and that I could be happy if he would just change. No, I would not feel loving toward someone who gave me an analogy like that as a way to point out my shortcomings. I would have probably reacted the same way he did, by helping me even less.

There were two really low points for me that let me know we had crossed the point of no return in our marriage. The first took place in the second house that we rented temporarily after the flood. It was an adjustment to settle in there, because the house was much smaller than Casa della Luna. The master bedroom had only one closet, so for the first time my husband and I had to share a closet—fun times. I had a lot more clothes than he did, and he resented that. It was just one more bit of evidence for him that I was the main cause of our discord. He felt I had way too many clothes, and he was right. He wanted me to be satisfied with owning three or four pairs of shoes as he did. In his mind, he was leading by example, but I wasn't following. His life, he felt, would be so much easier and so much less complicated if only I were less... everything, but most of all, less needy. Why did I need all those clothes? Why did I need a house? Why did I need two kids? And why did I need more than half of that closet?

So he made a point of spreading his clothes out on the clothes rod so that they took up exactly half of the available closet space. His four pairs of shoes were also lined up to get their justly deserved space on the floor. When I came in later to place my clothes and shoes in the closet, I knew exactly what the neatly and perfectly balanced placement of his clothes and shoes meant. It meant that he was feeling stressed and overwhelmed by this whole unplanned for adventure in living arrangements and wanted to point out that it was my fault. I too was stressed and feeling overwhelmed by our adventure, so I was immediately defensive. This was our way of dealing with stress. Instead of finding support and comfort in one another and feeling united in times like these, we each retreated into our own inner dialogue of how things were or were not. Unfortunately, the closet also had a relationship issue with regard to the clothes rod. The rod that was meant to hold the clothes was not installed properly. The brackets that were meant to support it were only screwed into the drywall. Once I hung my clothes, the rod collapsed under the added weight.

And there I was, once again in need of a champion: someone who could recognize my weakness and rescue me. I never tried to hide my weaknesses or my neediness. There was a perfect example all right there on the floor of that closet. Of course, I wanted my husband to come to my rescue and fix the situation with love and compassion. But the dialogue in my head was already telling me that he would not fix it, that he would be irritated with the request, and that he would look at all my things on the floor and see the "story of his life" with me. These thoughts that I had of his probable reaction did not keep me from wanting and hoping that he would fix the clothes rod. Just the opposite: they made me want him to fix it more—to prove me wrong, and to show me that he did not see me as an inconvenient burden that made his life less of whatever it is he wanted it to be. I wanted him to find joy in fixing that closet. I wanted him to reach out to me in this way and let me know he thought I was worth the trouble. That my presence made his life more of whatever it is he wanted it to be. So when I asked him to fix it, I'm sure all the angst I was feeling inside registered in my request. He may have heard this angst as criticism, as confirmation that I was oblivious to him and his worth as anything other than a means to my ends. At least that's what he was thinking in my mind.

I felt that it was his job to fix it even though, technically, I had broken it, and I definitely could have fixed it quite easily myself. But there was something in me that needed to feel that almost humiliating feeling of being disappointed by the man from whom I expected so much but who wanted to give me so little. So I asked my husband to fix the rod that he had nothing to do with breaking but was just using to highlight what he perceived as one of my weaknesses, with his insistence that he have half the space in that closet. He didn't create that weakness, nor could he fix it. But I asked him to anyway.

It was a loaded question. It was loaded with all the frustration that I had allowed to build up over the last two months. I had been doing everything I could to make sure our family had a roof over our heads, and that our children had everything they needed. All this I did while my husband waited for me to tell him what to do and occasionally complained that I didn't do something right. I was exhausted and wanted to find some place of refuge, even if it was temporary—even if it was in him taking care of me in this small way. He, filled with his own frustrations, begrudgingly agreed to fix it.

But, as trivial things sometimes can, this one incident triggered a fiasco I like to refer to as the closet war of 2015. Our time frame of when the closet should have been fixed differed. This caused my husband's passive-aggressive tendencies to kick in, which sent my neediness into overdrive. Fixing the closet meant he would have to make a trip to the home-improvement store, which he didn't like and didn't feel should be done on an impromptu basis. His resentment that I didn't want to wait another day to hang my clothes caused him to botch the job, not once but twice. So my clothes hit the floor twice more. Finally, while I was still asleep in bed the next morning, he decided to "fix it" again by hammering loudly and then haphazardly dropping tools on the bed so that they would "accidentally" hit my feet.

The second low point for me was the absolute lowest point of our marriage. While still in the second rental house, I was trying to get my daughter to clean her room when my husband came home and didn't like my tone. In front of me, he told her that she didn't have to listen to me. That was something I would never have expected. I thought that even when we didn't agree or get along, we would always respect each other's role as parents. I knew we had reached this low point because the discord between us had spilled into that hallowed ground of parenting. I could see that there was too much stuff beneath the surface of our family. How my husband and I felt about each other had become the center-piece of our family.

All that was wrong with our family was because of some short-coming in the other. We started out as one, especially with the children, but we had each gone our separate ways. We had grown so far apart that we could no longer recognize ourselves in each other. We couldn't see each other in our children any more either. This was the motivation for me to make a change for the better for all of us.

There it was. I grasped that sleeping under the same roof, in the same bed, with my children's father was not a pillar of our nuclear family. I could finally see a clear path to improving our family life. The negative aspects that had become part of our fam-ily structure could be eliminated by untying the husband role from the father role and the mother role from the wife role. If we could remove the disappointments, judgments, and need for validation from each other, my husband and I could parent without the pol-lution from our relationship. For us, the father and mother roles were the only ones that were critical to our nuclear family. Our children needed a mother and father. It would have been nice if we could have given them the gift of an example of strong, enduring love between a husband and wife, but that was not our forte.

One thing I want to make clear, the preceding example not-withstanding, is that the problems in my marriage were not caused by parenting conflicts. Quite the opposite: the problems in my marriage caused the parenting conflicts. This is one reason that nesting works for us. We took the cause of the conflicts out of the equation. Nesting is the way we parent now, which is basically how we parented before the conflicts of the marriage interfered with it.

CHAPTER 3

Ascension

● ● ●

What a liberation to realize that the 'voice in my head' is
not who I am. 'Who am I, then?' The one who sees that.

ECKHART TOLLE

THE ABILITY TO RISE ABOVE my ego and see beyond the limits
that society puts on us was essential to my ability to preserve our
nuclear family after my divorce. Once my ex-husband and I both
accepted that we would no longer be in the spousal or lover roles,
the negative undercurrents that had dogged us throughout our
marriage began to dissipate. I knew that my feelings of angst and
lack were not his issues to solve. He didn't cause me to feel dissatis-
fied. My reactions were my choice. He did things that would have
elicited similar reactions in most women. He was not innocent, but
neither was I. I was very critical of him at times, but his feelings
of inadequacy were not my responsibility to fix, and ultimately we
both created our own unhappiness. I think people who are successful at marriage know instinctively how to maintain responsibility for their own emotions and states of mind most of the time.
They don't make their spouses responsible for their happiness.

Understanding my part in the dissolution of my marriage was one thing, but the need to see my ex-husband differently was another.

Now I understood that my criticisms of him had little to do with him. They were my feeble attempts to get him to meet my needs so that I could feel validated and connected. It was humbling to accept that I could no longer make myself believe that I was the most important person in his life and one of the main focuses for the things he did or didn't do. Even when I was in the midst of my anger at him for letting me down, I sometimes glimpsed outside myself and saw that I was simply resisting my awareness that I was really asking him to crucify himself for me.

One of the issues that caused lots of negativity in our marriage was the great scout/music dichotomy. I encouraged my son to join Cub Scouts, because I thought it would be a great experience for him. My hope was that he would enjoy it so much that he would go on to become a Boy Scout. I understand now that my desire was ultimately for my own ego. But I'm human, and I have hopes and dreams for my kids as any other parent does. My husband didn't like anything about scouting. He didn't like camping out, and he thought the adults in scouting were weird. A big issue for him was giving up his free time doing something he didn't like or care about.

In the beginning, he attended scouting activities mainly because the camp-outs were family camp-outs when the boys were really young. But he never really participated; he just went along. I did all the planning, arranging, volunteering, and so on. That annoyed me because even though I knew how he felt about scouting, I thought that he would put in more effort because he loved me and because his son enjoyed it.

He didn't see things that way. Since he didn't see the value in scouting, he didn't see the value in participating. I was upset that he wouldn't do it anyway. I expected him to enjoy not the scouting, but the fact that he was doing something for me. It was a lot of work sometimes for me to keep up with some of the activities. I was often stretched pretty thin, and even a little more effort from him now and then would have made things a lot easier for me. Sometimes I would have to rush home from work on a Friday evening to pack for a camping trip. I remember once, after rushing home, packing, and making sure we had all the supplies we needed, we all piled into the truck ready to go, when my husband turned to me and asked me where to go. He hadn't even taken the initiative to figure out directions to the campground even though he would be driving. I saw it as a lack of compassion for me. One little small thing he could have easily taken off my plate. It was our differing opinions again on the definition of husband. To me, if a husband sees his wife carrying a heavy load, he tries to help her with it, even if he doesn't think she should be carrying that load. I saw his participation in scouting as an act of love for me. He would be making my life easier. Someone once told me that a husband should do what he can to make his wife's life easier, and that a wife should do the same for her husband: I had internalized that sentiment and made it part of my expectations of marriage. I thought that if he loved me, he would want to make my life easier.

Eventually, he just stopped participating all together. This didn't relieve him of my criticism, however; it exacerbated it, especially because I wasn't asking anything of him that I wouldn't do myself. For example, I participated from a "back seat" and let him direct our children's early education. They had the opportunity to go to a school for the gifted and talented that would have been more academically challenging and enriching for them than where they ended up going, but my husband, as a classically trained musician, wanted them to go to an elementary school where they would spend a large portion of their days having violin or cello lessons. I wanted them to go to the more academically challenging school, but my husband told me that learning music would be more enriching for them.

I knew that his desire to have them play instruments was as much about him as my wanting them in scouting was about me. But I told myself that since I loved and trusted him, and because he was more vested in the children learning to play instruments, it was an act of sacrificial love for me to support him in this. So I supported him completely. I even took the initiative at times to make sure they got as much out of their training as they could. I volunteered at their school when I could, and I sat through hours and hours of school concerts. I definitely would have rather been doing something else, but I never complained or acted put out by it.

This situation was the source of one of the many resentments I held on to for way too long. My husband held on to blaming me for his feelings of inadequacy for way too long. He would tell me, "Accept me as I am," which I heard as, "You're not worth the effort for me to do the things you want me to do," and that caused me to be even more needy and critical. It was this dynamic that led, at the highest point in our vicious cycle, to his most pervasive passive-aggressive way of dealing with my neediness, which he understood as criticism. When I expressed that I needed something from him, he often withheld it. That was his reaction to what he felt was unfair pressure for him to meet my needs. He felt that if I loved him, I would crucify myself for him by giving up what I desired and accept whatever he decided to give me or not. He felt that I shouldn't have expectations of him.

Neither of us had the skills to love in a way that didn't require the other to become a martyr. Our power struggle to get our needs met led to the ultimate demise of our marriage. We could not share our vulnerabilities with each other. We couldn't connect emotionally. We were too rigid, and there was no room for openness, kindness, or gentleness. We were on different wavelengths of needs, and we lacked the timing to meet each other's needs. And even though we had this ache of perpetual frustration in common, we couldn't find relief from it in each other. The more we wanted from each other, the less we gave. We shut each other down. There was an emptiness between us that was too dense for us to get through.

That didn't stop us from needing a connection, so we both looked elsewhere for it. We wanted to be around people who could see and hear us. It was painful to live physically with someone but to be isolated from that person at the same time. Connection is needed for the open flow of passionate energy and liveliness that turns a house into a home. My ex found islands of relief in connections outside the house. He found the passion, energy, and liveliness he craved in his music. In those relatively brief, bright moments, he stepped away from the crushing disappointment of not being good enough without sacrifice. He found a place where he could be vulnerable, and it wasn't in the house that I had named Casa della Luna.

I was committed to preserving the nuclear family for our children after our divorce. But in order for this to happen, I had to get my husband, the man I couldn't connect with enough to be married to, to agree with me. I already knew that he wouldn't participate in something simply because I thought it was a good idea. He had to sincerely agree that it was in his and the children's best interests. From my point of view, it was in the children's best interests, but I couldn't present it as a concrete fact.

We didn't simultaneously decide that divorce was the best option. I told him that I wanted a divorce before I told him that I wanted a nesting arrangement. His reaction was one I didn't expect. First he said he didn't want a divorce. I told him that it didn't matter; we would be divorced. He didn't resist that strongly; I think he was testing me to see if I was certain. Then he suggested it would be in the children's best interests for him to have primary custody. He implied that my style of parenting was not best for the children.

I wasn't ready for that, and I didn't react well. But I was already in a matter-of-fact mode, so I was able to maintain my composure, on the outside anyway. I calmly said, "We can fight about money, who did what to who, whatever. I'll be OK with that. But if you do anything to try and alienate me from my children, I will chop you up into little pieces and put you down the garbage disposal." Now I wish I had not said that. If he had said that to me, I probably would have gotten a restraining order against him. He and I both knew that I was not speaking literally, but it was a tone that had never existed between us until that moment. It was a glimpse of what it could be like if one of us were relegated to the "weekend parent" role. We could go from a bad marriage to an even worse divorce. Neither one of us wanted that. But we were both trying to lookout for ourselves so we were both on the defensive. What I perceived as his attempt to alienate me from my children was his attempt not to be alienated from his children. I also thought that his implication that the children should be primarily with him was simply a tactic that he was planning to use to his financial advantage. For him, it was a tactic he was trying so he would not be taken advantage of financially. I was no longer in a power struggle with him, so my need to criticize him diminished quickly. It allowed me to open myself to the possibility that maybe his motives weren't about me. I learned not to hold my negative thoughts about him in such high esteem. I understood that just because I thought something, it didn't make it true. This was the beginning of our new family.

CHAPTER 4

The Nest

• • •

Home is where you feel at home and are treated well.

DALAI LAMA

NESTING IS A CO-PARENTING ARRANGEMENT sometimes referred to as "bird's-nest" parenting. In this arrangement, the children live in the family home and the parents move in and out, "like birds alighting and departing a 'nest.' During the time parents are not at home with the kids, they live in a separate dwelling, which can either be on their own or rotated with the other parent" (Kruk 2013). The house that the children live in is often referred to as the nest, in these situations.

My husband and I agreed that it would be best for the children to spend equal time with both of us after the divorce. After having had to move them twice due to the Memorial Day flood that profoundly changed our lives, we wanted to provide them with as much stability as we could. For us, that meant we would find a place for them to live peacefully, where connections were easy and energy flowed unimpeded by the complicated dynamics that had controlled our marriage. We wanted a place where they could possibly live until they were ready to live on their own. We decided to make it happen.

With that decision, things seemed to line up easily to make nesting a reality. The responsibility for the planning and carrying out of this decision was mine, primarily because I had the vision and secondarily because my ex didn't want the responsibility. He was content to have me tell him what he needed to do. I didn't add this to my list of grievances about him as I would have if we had stayed married. Now I felt that it was my contribution to the higher good. I didn't want to keep score. I didn't need to. I was good at planning and organizing and this was my family, so I would be tenacious in my pursuit of what I thought was best for all of us.

My ex-husband also gave selflessly of himself to make this happen. He was generous in his financial support of this arrangement. He could just as easily have opted for the default role that many fathers take after divorce. He could have started a new life and been content with seeing his children every other weekend. No one would have faulted him for that.

We both did what we could to the best of our abilities. It didn't matter anymore who did what. Neither of us had anything to prove any longer. I didn't feel the need to ask him to do something for me just to make me feel loved. If it was something I could do myself, I did it, and I loved myself for doing it. I was all grown up now. My ex no longer held back just to prove that he was worth more than what he could do for me. He found his own initiative. I did what needed to be done, and I accepted him as he was for who he was: the imperfect father of my children.

I wrote our divorce decree and the parenting plan that was filed with it. We didn't use attorneys or mediators. I would have preferred to use a mediator, but my ex-husband didn't want to have other input into our plans if we could avoid it. We only had difficulty agreeing on things a few times, but we ultimately agreed on all issues. Considering how we were when we were married, this was a testament to our motivation to make the arrangement work. The parenting plan I created was drafted from an example I found online ("Sample Parenting Agreement" n.d.).

Our parenting agreement gives each one of us primary custody of our children in alternating two-week intervals until our youngest reaches the age of eighteen. There is no particular reason why I chose two weeks as the interval; it just seemed workable and long enough to not feel like we were living in a revolving door. The agreement states that we switch every other Sunday at five o'clock, but in actuality we usually switch between noon and two. My ex-husband gets up early for work, so he likes to be settled in pretty early. There have also been times when we switched a day or so early. Once when I went camping with my son, my ex came to the nest early to stay with my daughter, and another time, my ex wanted to take the children out of town to visit relatives. Also in the parenting plan, we agreed that no unrelated people over the age of eighteen would be allowed to stay overnight at the nest. The plan also requires that the non-nesting parent should live within two miles or fifteen minutes from the nest.

Whoever is nesting with the children is to be responsible for all the parenting duties: all the care and feeding, extracurricular activities, and so on. However, I still take my son to his Boy Scout meetings even if I'm not nesting. I don't mind, and I don't hold it against my ex. I also took him to most of his baseball games and practices, even though my ex helped if I needed it.

Not everything that is important to us and how we live is included in the parenting agreement. That would have made it too long and more likely to cause problems, because it would probably have made us feel like we couldn't just figure out things on the fly as they came up. For example, we also have two dogs that live at the nest. I take care of all their needs because my ex, even though he likes them, said that if he had gotten primary custody of the kids, he would not have taken the dogs. I sort of understand. He was never a dog person, and when my son asked for a pet, I, being a dog person, decided to get him a dog. My ex was adamantly against it. He told me that if I got a dog, he would divorce me. I got two: one for my daughter and one for my son. I didn't do it just to spite their father. I only wanted one, but there were only two dogs left in the litter when I arrived to pick up the girl puppy. Her brother, who was very attached to her, had a severe underbite, and I feared no one would take him.

Our children love their dogs. At the time of our divorce, they had been a part of our family for five years. If it had come down to my ex having primary custody of the children, I know he would have stood by his pronouncement that he would not take the dogs. In my mind, I think the kids would have accepted that from him, and they would not have held it against him. I would have taken the dogs and probably let him know on a regular basis how wrong I thought he was not to take them. The way it turned out, the dogs nest also. This is just an example of an issue that could have caused discord, but I chose to let it be, and I just take care of the dogs.

The financial arrangement for the expense of the nest was the subject of a major negotiation. After taking into consideration my ex-husband's aversion to home ownership and my aversion to renting, I determined that it would be best for me to purchase the house we now use as the nest. When our nesting arrangement is finished, I will likely sell the house. I also paid to have an additional master suite (see chapter 5) added to it because I didn't want to share a bedroom or bathroom with my ex, even if we would never be there at the same time. After considering everyone's needs, I decided where the nest should be located. I found the house I liked, and I bought it. I didn't ask for my ex's opinion. I also considered buying a duplex for us to share, but, in the end I decided against it because I wanted to respect our divorce. Living together, even if separated by a thick wall, seemed like an entanglement.

I purchased the nest and pay all the expenses relating to it. I'm not an attorney, so my understanding of the laws in Texas may not be completely accurate, but I'm under the impression that one person has to be named as primary guardian of the children. That person has the right to decide where the children will live. So, according to our divorce decree, I am number one when it comes to deciding where the children live, but that is not the spirit of our agreement. However, in order to make our financial arrangements official, we chose to make me the custodial parent, and my ex-husband pays me child support, even though the children live with each of us equally.

This works for us because my ex-husband doesn't like home-ownership or the hassle of taking care of a house. He prefers renting and leaving the bother to someone else. I'm the opposite. I like owning where I live, so I purchased the nest and the house I live in when I'm not at the nest. If I want to dig up the backyard and put in a koi pond, I don't want to have to ask permission. As for the everyday items like food and incidentals, whichever parent is nesting is responsible for those things.

The result of all the planning and actions was the continuation of our nuclear family after our divorce. The undercurrents of irritation, frustration, and anger that plagued Casa della Luna were washed away in the receding waters of Brays Bayou. The nest is a house where we can all find room to be vulnerable. We can be ourselves. There is room for passion, energy, and liveliness.

Connections are made, and the life that is being lived in the nest has undercurrents of love, joy, and peace.

Our nest is quite different from our old house. It's only half the size, and it's not in a trendy neighborhood, as Casa della Luna was. The yard is too small and shaded to grow vegetables, which was one of my hobbies at the old house. Yet I love being at the nest and so do the kids. It has a nice feel to it, and it also has a good heart. The life that is being lived inside it is strong, and it makes that house a home. It is the centerpiece of our nesting arrangement.

The nest is where the children reside 100 percent of the time. It is the base where each parent has time with the children. That parent can interact and make rules and exceptions to rules as he or she sees fit. Of course, the children are free to contact the non-nesting parent anytime they want to, and the non-nesting parent can interact with the children at any time.

I've considered making our two-week parenting time longer as the children get older, but two weeks seems to be the right amount of time for us at present. In our situation, we both still see the children practically every day. I drive them both to school, and my ex-husband takes them home, regardless of who's at the nest. This was not planned in our parenting agreement; it just happened to work out that way because of our work schedules.

As far as cleaning, both my ex-husband and I try to leave the house (besides the kids' rooms) in relatively good order when it's time to switch. I still do most of the cleaning. My ex never cleans the children's rooms, nor does he make them do it. I don't complain. He can parent the way he likes. We both attend all school functions whenever they arise. I usually stay informed about grades and schoolwork; if something needs attention while the children's father is nesting, I'll let him know, and he will take action if really necessary. I will pay for any extracurricular activities they do, whether I think they should do them or not. Their father only pays for things he supports. For example, my son wanted to play little-league baseball when he was eleven, the last year he was eligible. He had never really played beyond age three or four. His father didn't think it was a good idea for him to play at age eleven because he already had too many extra things to do—mainly music and scouting. So he didn't pay for anything to do with baseball, nor did he take him to practice unless I specifically asked. I did invite my ex to all our son's games, and he came to most of them. My ex also doesn't pay for scouting. He does pay for half of anything related to music. I will ask him if he wants to split the cost of certain things. If he says no, then I instantly drop it, and that's the end of it. His unwillingness to pay for anything for the kids that he doesn't agree with is part of nesting. It's part of the freedom of it. You can parent without judgment. It's like the First Amendment: you love it, but sometimes it has unfortunate consequences.

Our nesting schedule doesn't consider holidays. We didn't allow for any special arrangements for those days. Whichever parent has the kids on that holiday has them. Our parenting agreement did state that exceptions can be made to the custody schedule, as long as both parents agree. So far, we have made such agreements. I allowed my ex to take the children to Dallas the day after Thanksgiving even though I was nesting. My ex let me start my turn early on Mother's Day.

Working together has been relatively easy, even though we've had a few disagreements. Once, my daughter broke her expensive cell phone just a couple of months after I replaced a prior expensive cell phone that she lost. I decided that part of the cost of the new phone would come out of her allowance. My daughter thought that it was unfair, so she complained to her father, who told me that it wasn't fair. At that point, I took the phone away and told him he could buy her one then. The disagreement deteriorated pretty quickly, and my ex and I found ourselves fighting about things that had happened in our marriage. Once I realized that was happening, I retreated and gave her back the phone. I remembered what was important. What was important was that they got to experience both their parents in a setting where they can make real emotional connections with them.

Explaining our nesting arrangement to people has been interesting. I think for the most part, our transition from traditional family living to nesting has been transparent. I didn't tell my family that my husband and I were divorced until we were already well into nesting. My ex had stopped attending my family functions years before, so it wasn't hard. Some of my relatives were upset that I didn't tell them I was getting a divorce because they believed they could have counseled us and prevented it from happening. That's exactly why I didn't tell them.

My husband got custody of our church, which was not a hard decision. He was more involved there at the time, and I had outgrown it. He still took the children to church with him until my daughter announced that she no longer wanted to go.

My son had always been a bit indifferent about going to church. I remember when he was four, overhearing him tell his sister, "You know God is not real; that's just something they tell us." He enjoyed it when he did go. He had friends there and he participated in ushering and whatever else he was asked to do. He was a bit squeamish about singing in the children's choir, but he did it until he realized one Sunday that he was the only boy in that choir. I think his approach was since he had to go, he would make it worth his while. His temperament is closer to his father's. He'll decide what's what. When he was three, I decided it was time to teach him how to read. I called him into his bedroom so that he could watch me put alphabet stickers on his mirror. I told him that I was going to teach him how to read. His response changed the way I approach my children with any of my desires for them going forward. He said, "If you put those stickers on my mirror, I'm going to run away from home." I was stunned. I did not put the stickers on the mirror, and I don't know how he learned to read, but he does it quite well now.

My daughter, on the other hand, had started out as a strong believer. When she was very young, maybe three, I told her once that I was going to "tell God" about some small infraction she had committed. She was immediately contrite. I was slightly surprised that she responded to that so quickly. I could use that or "Santa Claus is watching," and it worked like a charm until she started school. Then she started to challenge just about everything. I could feel her sense of pride when she told me that she was no longer a Christian. I told her it was too late, she had already been confirmed and I witnessed it. I told her it was like being a Texan, once you are one, that's it. I told her, "Even if you don't go to church, you will be a Christian; you'll just be considered a lost sheep." She's still pondering that one.

My close friends, my inner circle, probably knew that we were divorcing before I did. They were skeptical at first about the nesting arrangement, but they applauded it once they saw it in action. The parents of my children's friends were more confused than anything. They never knew whom to call when they wanted to know if someone could pick up their children from school or if there was a party or something. Prior to our divorce, I handled all that. I knew all the mothers, and we had exchanged favors all through our kids' schooling. At first, if my ex was nesting, I had them call him to make arrangements or ask if the kids were available. But that soon became too cumbersome, and one mom even said outright that she never knew whom to call, implying her frustrations. At that point I decided to relieve them of the burden of trying to keep track of our schedule. The relationships with the parents were primarily with me anyway. So I took over handling my children's social arrangements for the most part. But now that they are teenagers, they do most of it themselves anyway. I'm just the chauffeur.

Our arrangement allows the children to have lives that are uninterrupted by frequent weekends away from their home base. They have a place for all their favorite things and to have their friends over. Having to live in two places, I can really appreciate that. There's no need to consider what activities they can do with which parent. The nest is a place where everyone has space, and there is no emptiness that cannot be reached across.

One thing that I'm still getting used to is that the house itself is only a temporary dwelling place for us. Once my youngest is an adult, we won't need it. Even though the flood taught me that a house is only sticks and bricks, I still have a twinge for the lost dream of a family homestead.

A nest is, first of all, functional. Its function is to have the children live in one residence. Our arrangement allows my ex and I to have our own space in the nest, which I consider a blessing. We can go weeks without laying eyes on each other, and we like it that way. The nest allows each of us to parent without interference from the children's other parent. How each parent arranges the children's lives while "nesting" with the children is up to that parent, and the non-nesting parent has no input unless asked. It's a place for traditions to be made and continued. The traditions can be unique to each parent or they can include the other parent, but it is still the domain of the nesting parent.

CHAPTER 5

Two Masters

● ● ●

If you want to bring an end to long-standing
conflict, you have to be prepared to compromise.

AUNG SAN SUU KYI

RIGHT AFTER I PURCHASED THE nest, I had another master suite
built onto it so that I could have my own space. At first, the plan
was for my ex and me to share the one master bedroom. But the
more I thought about it, the more I didn't want to share a closet,
much less a bedroom, with him. Even if we were never there at the
same time, his essence would be there. It would be residue from
our marriage.

The space between us that had caused me so much pain before
had become my refuge. I could only be free in my own space. It's
funny how something I loathed in one context, I craved in another.
I wanted to make the transition every two weeks as seamless as
possible. We didn't have to be so strict with time that overlapping
would cause problems. If he forgot something and needed to come
back to the nest to get it, he wouldn't disturb my refuge. We, not
the children, shoulder the burden of living in more than one place.

That is the crux of the nesting arrangement: lightening the burden of divorce on the children.

In the beginning, the switching between two living places was sort of a drag. I hadn't yet figured out that I didn't have to have two of everything or pack up a lot of stuff each week. The house I live in when I'm not at the nest is close enough that I can go there to get something if I need it. Also, I found that when I'm nesting, I usually go to my other house to get ready for work after I drop the kids off at school. It's just easier. Little things like that have helped me get used to the switch-up. But I still sometimes drive to the wrong house after work.

I live at the nest with the children 50 percent of the time. When I'm there, I run the house in much the same way as I did when I was married. I cook dinner most nights, and the children and I eat together. A lot of our connecting happens during that time, during the cooking, eating, and cleaning up afterward. I sometimes give the kids chores to do, but I'm not that strict about it. If there is homework, I cajole them into doing it.

The improvement is that I can interact with my children without my ex-husband's critical input. It was not always an issue between us; it only became an issue near the end of our marriage. However, now that our children are teenagers, interacting with them can be a delicate dance. Because my ex-husband and I aren't attuned to each other enough, trying to address issues with the children together can be disastrous.

My daughter was very stressed during her freshman year of high school, as it was turning out to be more demanding than she had anticipated. She loved her school, but she was having a hard time keeping up with the rigorous workload. I hired a tutor who came by the nest once a week to help her with her French. The tutor wanted to review my daughter's tests to see what she needed help with. My daughter couldn't find the papers in her room because it was so messy and she has real issues with organization. I went into her room, irritated that she had given up what I considered to be too easily, and found the papers for her. Then, while she was with the tutor, I cleaned up her room.

That was enough to push her over the edge. She was overwhelmed and emotional and verbally lashed out at me. I don't allow my children to raise their voices to me, so I knew this meant that she was really having trouble. I told her to go cool off in her room. After a few minutes, I went into her room, lay across her bed, and stroked her hair. I was able to show her tenderness so that she would feel safe expressing herself in a more tempered way. I let her tell me what she was feeling, and she expressed all her recent frustration. In the end, I held her and told her that I loved her and would do whatever I could to help her be successful in school. I let her know that if she brought a problem to me, I would listen to her and do what she needed me to do to help her.

I'm convinced that if my ex-husband had been there, her initial outburst would have compelled him to come to her rescue. Then the focus would have turned onto me and what I had done to upset her. That would have triggered our cycle, and my daughter would have been lost in the abyss between her father and me. She would have likely retreated to her room while her father and I spent the next hour criticizing each other's parenting skills. She would not have gotten the understanding and comforting she needed at that moment. I probably would not have found out what was really stressing her—her schoolwork. Her father would have interpreted the situation as me being what was stressing her. He would have comforted her for having to put up with such an inconsiderate mother, as he had had to put up with his father. He probably would have told her that she didn't have to worry—he wouldn't let me clean her room anymore if she didn't want me to.

I love nesting.

This doesn't mean that my ex-husband and I never parent together. We do. I have often put him on speakerphone so that he could support me in encouraging our children in something. I also put him on speakerphone every three months or so, when my daughter asks if she can have a kitten. He's my "ace in the hole" for that one. Fortunately, we agree: no more animals at the nest.

One thing concerned me when we first started nesting. My daughter had fallen into the role of "woman of the house" when I wasn't there. I didn't get all the details, but I saw this on a few occasions during the transition. As soon as my ex walked into the house, my daughter said, "Come on, Dad; we need to go to the grocery store." She was clearly in charge. I didn't say anything, because I didn't know how I felt about it at first. I ultimately decided that it was none of my business. Different people parent in different ways. I know my ex wasn't forcing her to take responsibility for running things. He's not that kind of dad. He was just letting her because she did it naturally, and he didn't mind because it helped him. I admire both of them for working together like that. However, the novelty of getting to plan meals and get things for the house seems to have worn off for my daughter. She lets her father do it all now. I think it was sort of like when she first "wanted" to wash dishes.

Even though my ex and I are good at staying out of each other's parenting, we still feel each other's influence. Since I own the nest and pay all the bills, I decide what Internet and television service there is at the nest and how those things are used. My ex-husband defers to me on all things electronic and technical. With two teenagers in the house, that's a big deal. I had to resort to automating most things; my ex-husband is usually in bed by seven thirty because he goes to work so early. This meant the kids would stay up way too late, and he wouldn't even know it. I could see when they were online or on their phones, and I told my ex, but he didn't know how to stop them. Now I turn the Internet off at a certain time through an app on my phone. I also use an app to lock their cell phones at certain times.

My ex-husband and I also differ on how we teach our kids about the world. I take the kids on a week's vacation at least once a year. That's important to me. My ex doesn't travel with the kids except to visit relatives. We also differ in our philosophies about how they should interact civically. I like them to be in scouts, to know their neighbors, and to explore where they live. My ex doesn't believe they need to be taught things like that. He is, however, much more cautious about their general safety. He doesn't want the children to explore our neighborhood or city alone. He believes it's too dangerous. So when he is nesting, they are not allowed to go far from the nest without him. When I am nesting, I encourage them to walk the two or three blocks to the store by themselves to buy a school supply they are missing. I've even let them walk to a nearby restaurant to have dinner on their own when I've had to work late. We had the same issues about the kids walking to school. Our son's school is only three-quarters of a mile from the nest—just a fifteen-minute walk. I think he should walk to school most days and be driven only if the weather is bad. My ex-husband disagrees. He thinks it's too dangerous because our son has to cross a major intersection. I respect his concern, so I drive my son to school most mornings. I just think my son is missing something. The walk is a possibility to interact with life. It could be an adventure!

Ultimately, our nesting lives look pretty much the way they would have if my ex and I could have stayed married and connected with each other. We are both so much more at ease with each other now. There were some incidents in the beginning that challenged us. A main one had to do with finances. At first, my ex thought he was contributing more than was necessary. He knew that if we did it the traditional way, with me being the primary parent and him having the children every other weekend and thirty days in the summer, he would be paying a lot less in child support. I'm convinced that it is worth the extra cost for him. And I actually contribute more than he does to our arrangement. When we were married, he basically gave me everything he earned to run the household, and I added whatever else I needed to from my income. Now, he gives me half of what he used to give me, but I have kept our children's lifestyle basically the same. That means I have to pick up more of the costs. However, I do own the house, and if the housing market is favorable when the kids leave the nest, I will hopefully be able to sell it, which will have a positive impact on my finances.

Another thing I have come to understand is that I must consider the source before I heed the advice of friends and family. Even though I know that my friends and loved ones have my best interest at heart, I need to thoroughly vet any advice they give me. I can never substitute their judgment for mine, even if what they are advising seems reasonable. I "eat the fish and spit out the bones." When people give advice, they usually will give it based on their own experiences. I must make decisions based on my experiences, not theirs.

I was talking to a friend when the topic of school supplies came up. I told her how much I spent to get my daughter what she needed. It was more than I had expected to spend. My friend asked if my ex would be paying for half of the supplies. I said no, I didn't mind paying for all the supplies myself. We had just started nesting and things were going smoothly, so I didn't want to start, what I considered, would be nitpicking. My friend thought that I should ask my ex to pay for half the school supplies. She thought it was important to set the right precedent. It really wasn't important to me that everything be split fifty-fifty. My ex and I had generally the same temperament with money; we didn't keep exacting tabs. We never made, or stuck to, budgets. We were both pretty freewheeling when it came to small things like I considered school supplies to be. But, I thought, my friend has a point. So I called my ex and asked him to pay for half of our daughter's school supplies. We argued about it for two hours! When we were about fifteen minutes in, I realized that I had made a mistake and that this was not a fight I wanted to have. But I had already thrown down the gauntlet. I persevered, and he agreed to reimburse me for half the cost of the school supplies. I later was talking to another friend about the school supplies incident, and she asked me why I would take advice from my other friend, who had never been married. That helped me understand that even though my ex and I are divorced, we still must negotiate with one another quite often. Married couples do it all the time. After years of such negotiations, you get to know the other person well and their traits, good and bad, aren't going to change just because you are divorced.

Our parenting agreement does obligate both my ex and me to pay for the children's college educations if they choose to pursue them, but my ex has indicated that he is not inclined to do so. He and I both paid for our own educations, so I understand his position. However, if he ultimately decides not to contribute financially to their college educations, then I will have to figure out how to pay for them without him. Even though the agreement is binding, I would not enforce that part of it. That's the spirit of nesting. Both parents are allowed to decide what is important for them to do or not do for their children.

We have definitely found our rhythm with this parenting arrangement. Things run smoothly most of the time. If something throws things out of kilter, my ex and I are centered enough that we are now comfortable working it out together. We have let go of our expectations of one another; we accept whatever the other one brings to the table, and we are grateful for it. We know that we are both working for the benefit of our children. We try not to bring our egos to the nest.

It's hard for me to imagine what it would have been like if one of us had insisted on being primary guardian for the children and relegating the other to basically being a spectator in the children's lives. I never wanted to be a single parent. I don't think most people want to. It's usually the second choice or a last resort. But more than not wanting to have to handle the daily care and feeding of my children on my own was my desire to provide a two-parent home for them to be receive the benefits that both their parents have for them.

The nest for us is more than just the sticks and bricks that make up the house that we live in. It's home and hearth for all of us. The hearth is the heart of the home, the center that we all find comfort in and draw strength from. It's the life that is being lived inside the house that makes it a home. And our hearth is alive with energy, connection, and liveliness. It may have taken us a while to get to this point, but we can finally say we made it. We took the long scenic route to home. We are truly a family now, and it's the family I've always wanted.

CHAPTER 6

The Farm

● ● ●

Peace is not absence of conflict, it is the ability
to handle conflict by peaceful means.

RONALD REAGAN

WHEN I'M NOT AT THE nest, I'm at the farm. That's what I named
my personal house because of my propensity for growing edibles.
This is where I plan to live out the rest of my time here on earth.
It is a nice, cozy place that's only two miles from the nest. In the
beginning, it was difficult for me to get a feeling of home when
I was at the farm. It took some time before I found my rhythm
with the two-week switch-up. I always looked forward to being
with them again. That dynamic made going back to the farm
anticlimactic.

The two-weeks-on and two-weeks-off situation also limits my
options for making the farm cozier. I would normally have a pet,
more plants, and more interactions with my neighbors. I can't have
a pet at the farm because I'm not living there half the time. The
children's dogs can live at the nest because someone is always there.
Also, it's more complicated getting to know my neighbors because

I have fewer opportunities to bump into them, and then I have to explain why I'm not there half the time. I don't mind explaining nesting to new people; it's just that people often don't really get it, and I just get a blank stare in return for my explanation.

The proximity to the nest is important because it makes handling routine and unexpected things a lot easier, like picking up the kids each morning for school, which, as I've mentioned, I do even when I'm not nesting. Also, being close is a must in case of emergencies. My son once texted me at around nine at night to tell me that my ex was taking my daughter to the emergency room because she had been stung by a puss-moth caterpillar. My son even texted me a link to a website explaining what the implications were for being stung by a puss-moth caterpillar. What I read on the website left me with the impression that a trip to the emergency room was not necessary. I called my son, and he told me about a kid at his school who was bitten by a puss-moth caterpillar and had to be hospitalized for weeks. Sure. He's in middle school. I think that in Texas, middle school is when they start teaching boys how to tell those infamous "tall tales." I wasn't really too concerned because I know my daughter has a real fear of bugs, so it was likely that my ex was taking her to the ER just to calm her down. I had never heard of anyone dying from a caterpillar sting.

I called my ex to find out what was going on, and it's a good thing I did. He was driving around, looking for the children's hospital and its emergency room. He couldn't find it. We had been there several times over the years for various cuts that needed stitching and even broken bones that needed attention. So I was puzzled as to why he couldn't find it, and even more so about why he was looking for the big show that was the children's hospital. Maybe he was just driving around to give my daughter a chance to say she didn't really need to see a doctor. I knew that wouldn't happen. I told him it would probably be easier and faster if he went to one of those "doc-in-a-box" places. He took my advice, and I met him there.

They saw my daughter and determined that she was not having an allergic reaction. They gave her a prescription for pain medication that she didn't want to have filled because, by the time we left, she couldn't even pinpoint where she came into contact with the bug. I split the cost of the emergency room visit with my ex, even though I probably wouldn't have taken her to the emergency room. But it was his call.

The farm has three bedrooms. Even though I live alone and would have done well with a smaller house, I hope that my children will one day consider the farm their home. I imagine that once they leave the nest and want to "come home" for visits, it will be to the farm. They may even want to live there for a while after college. I hope that they will see my home as their home.

When we first started nesting, I was reluctant to bring my children to the farm to visit with them. I wasn't sure if that would make them feel less like the nest was their—our—real home. I wanted to give them time to bond with the nest. They knew I lived somewhere else when I wasn't with them, but I didn't know how they felt about it. After a while, I realized that they didn't really think about what I was doing or where I was when I wasn't with them. They were with their dad at those times, and I suppose it was like I just went out to run some errands or hang out with my friends. They didn't pine for me when I wasn't there, and that was a good thing.

My ex-husband chooses to live in a one-bedroom apartment when he's not nesting. He likes to keep things simple. I don't know what he'll do when the kids leave the nest and want to visit with him. Maybe he'll do that at his mother's house while she's still around.

Now that I understand that my kids don't feel anything unpleasant about me having another home, I do bring them to the farm sometimes. We celebrated New Year's Eve there this year because of our tradition of building a fire and setting off fireworks. The farm has a bigger yard and no neighbors behind it, so it's better for those festivities. We have had a tradition of fire and sparklers and a family snapshot on New Year's Eve for as long as my children remember. Now that I am divorced, I continue the tradition with the children, as it was my creation. However, it's getting harder to keep them interested. Last year, my daughter was on her phone with her friends during the festivities. This year, I relented and let her celebrate with her friends after an abbreviated family celebration. I knew this would happen eventually, but I wanted to continue as many family traditions for as long as I could.

What happens at the farm stays at the farm. I hadn't lived alone in fifteen years. I quickly realized that a residual benefit of nesting is the time I got to spend living alone, doing things I enjoyed, without having to concern myself as much with what the children were doing. This aspect of nesting should make it appealing to lots of people. I get to recharge, and then when I am parenting, I have a lot more patience, and I think I do a much better job at it than I would if I didn't have those periods alone. I get to do whatever I want to without guilt. When I'm not nesting, I'm still a parent, so there are some self-imposed limitations for what happens at the farm. In case of emergency, the farm may need to become the children's "nest." I always keep that in mind.

I have gone on vacation during my non-nesting time. It was during the summer, when I didn't have to take the kids to school. I did let my ex know, although with cell phones, I probably didn't need to do so. It was just a courtesy, not a requirement. But if he needed help with something, he should know that I wouldn't be right around the corner for a few days.

Before I found the farm, my ex suggested I purchase the house next door, as it happened to be for sale. I quickly declined. I don't think it would have been a problem if I lived next door, but I prefer privacy; I'm a single woman now. Besides, I think it would be too tempting for the children to come next door if they couldn't find something in their rooms.

The freedom of nesting rejuvenates me and makes my parenting time better. When I'm living away from the nest, I garden, read, and entertain girlfriends, and I have even occasionally dated. I could do all these things if I lived with my children full time, but this way, I can do it when it's convenient for me—even on a school night.

The subject of dating while nesting often comes up in my conversations with others. One of my girlfriends asked me what would happen if I met someone whom I wanted to marry. I told her that I really didn't think I would be ready to marry anyone until my children were out of the nest. But I'm a realist, and I know that things happen. I told her that if I did meet someone I wanted to marry, he would have to be willing to accommodate my living with him for two weeks and then my living with my children for two weeks. I would not include him in the nesting arrangement, even though the way the agreement is written, I could. I wouldn't want to deal with that dynamic. I wouldn't be having any other children, so that would not be an issue at all. I do date sometimes, but I'm a hopeless romantic.

Dating while nesting in my age range has been interesting. I'm in my early fifties, and the men whom I would consider dating are my age or older. None of the ones I have gone out with has children living at home. They are usually caught a little off guard by the fact that I do. A couple of the men let me know that they didn't want to date a woman with minor children, even if they only lived with her half the time. I can't say I blame them. I wouldn't date a man with minor children. It would seem complicated, even though, for me, it's really not. I do find that dating and parenting at the same time can be tricky. For one, I'm just not as available. I prefer to only date when I'm at the farm. I have let my children know that I date, but they have never met anyone I've dated. I'm lucky that I don't have to even consider involving my kids in my dating life. I wouldn't involve them unless I was just about ready to marry someone, and that's unlikely. But I do enjoy the company of a nice man every now and again, so if the stars align and I meet someone special, I will definitely entertain him at the farm.

I know that I am beyond blessed to be able to maintain a home for my children with my ex-husband in such a way that they get the full benefit of both parents' time and resources at an equal level. After we had nested for a full year, I asked my children how they felt about it. All they said was "fine." Well, of course, they are children, and this family is the only one they have. They have nothing to compare it to except the families of their peers. The majority of their friends' parents are still married, but they do have friends whose parents are divorced, and those friends only live with one of the parents.

I know that my children would have been fine if my ex-husband and I could not have made this arrangement and they only could have lived with one of us. My concern would be that whichever parent was relegated to every other weekend and thirty days in the summer would quickly become disenfranchised. We both love our children and would do anything for them, but alienation happens, and I think nesting was the best thing we could have done to keep that from happening. I am grateful to my ex-husband for being open to living this way. He didn't have to be, and there is no law in Texas that would make nesting mandatory—but I think there should be.

CHAPTER 7

The Law

● ● ●

Change your thoughts and you change your world.

NORMAN VINCENT PEALE

NESTING IS THOUGHT TO HAVE originated in Virginia in 2000 with a divorce case that involved parents of two children ages three and five (Flannery 2004). In this case, a bird's-nest custody arrangement was made in which the children remained in the marital home with the mother during the week and with the father on the weekends. This instance of nesting was imposed on the couple by the judge. The father appealed this decision, contending that the trial court erred by failing to grant him an equal amount of time with the children each week. His appeal was denied.

In Texas, the state where I live, joint or sole custody is determined according to the best interests of the child. There is a default custody-and-visitation schedule that is set by the court if parents can't agree on visitation and custody themselves. It's the only option judges have.

A default standard custody order gives the noncustodial parent visitation and/or possession on every other weekend and for thirty days in the summer. This is accepted as an option that is best for the children. Now that we live in an age where we strive for equality in all things, equality in parenting is an idea whose time has come. I think there should be a standard nesting order included in Texas family law. All things considered (see chapter 8), nesting is a feasible option for parenting that should be considered after divorce.

My ex-husband and I maintain a total of three homes, but that is a luxury. We could have opted to only have one home, the nest, and then rented an apartment that we would have shared. That situation might have been even less expensive than not nesting.

In my divorce, I represented myself and my ex-husband in court. We did not use attorneys or a mediator. I will credit the wealth of information I gleaned from the Internet for that. I also credit my naïveté for presuming that the judge who signed our divorce decree would do so. She didn't have to. When the judge, Alyssa Lemkuil, who had been serving on the family court for less than two weeks, signed our parenting agreement along with our divorce decree, she said, "If y'all agree to this mess, I'll sign it." She was an attorney who was appointed to the newly formed 507th Judicial District (Family Court) in Houston by Governor Abbott. I don't know if others in Texas have attempted to have nesting agreements like mine approved by the court, but I would like other like-minded parents to know that it is possible. Nesting needs a national champion. There can be more support for parents who choose to nest in the form of tax incentives, public approval, and other accommodations. Marriage counselors can advocate nesting even for parents who aren't ready to divorce. Child advocates should support nesting as the preferred postdivorce parenting arrangement.

There is a wealth of information about postdivorce parenting; however, at the time that I am writing this book, there is very little about nesting. The experts who have weighed in on the subject have overwhelmingly said that nesting as a parenting plan isn't a good idea. These were mainly attorneys. I'm glad I didn't find those opinions before I wrote my agreement.

CHAPTER 8

The Way

● ● ●

If you don't like something, change it. If you
can't change it, change your attitude.

MAYA ANGELOU

THE NUMBER-ONE RESPONSE TO MY nesting arrangement is that it
must be expensive for us. Yes, it is. My ex-husband and I are not
typical. We are older, and we are both professionals. We maintain
a total of three homes, but that is a luxury.

Most of the documented arguments I know of for why nesting won't work come from a study by Reena Sommer (2012), as
follows:

- "Incurring the shared costs of the family home together
  with the costs of running a separate residence during non-
  parenting time."

This is also the number-one reason I've read for why nesting won't
work. I understand that it is a powerful one. Given the fact that
finances are often the cause of divorce, coming to agreement about

them afterward seems like a long shot. However, when couples divorce, they are forced to maintain two residences anyway. Both will need to accommodate the children. With nesting, only one residence needs to be large enough to accommodate children. The second home could be shared by the parents during their non-nesting time. My ex-husband and I could have opted to only have one home, the nest, and then rented an apartment that we would have shared. That situation might have been even less expensive than not nesting.

To make it even more economical, the co-parents can live with relatives, such as their own parents, when it is feasible. One of my sisters lives alone, not too far from our nest. I probably could have made arrangements to share a home or apartment with her if I wanted to make this arrangement more affordable for myself. The point is, with creativity, the people making the arrangements can find all sorts of ways to make nesting economical. And in most cases, the nesting parents would not have to see each other at all.

* "Higher utility bills during one parent's time at the family home."

Yes, it's likely that one parent will run the nest more frugally than the other. No matter how you slice it, there will be inequities. This will come down to the state of the relationship between the parents. If there is still unresolved anger, resentment, blame, disappointment, or even an unshared desire to reunite, nesting might not work. The last thing a nest should be is a battlefield.

The finances of the nest should be spelled out in the parenting agreement as much as possible. In my agreement, I am the one who pays all the bills for the nest. I'm pretty laid back when it comes to household expenses. If you asked me how much my electricity bill was, I couldn't tell you. I don't worry about turning off the lights or who forgot to turn the water off in the kitchen sink. For me, life is too short to sweat the small stuff. But I understand that some people do, and it makes their lives better because they are better with money. Got it.

There are measures those parents can take to make sure the other parent isn't taking things for granted. Smart meters can track electricity usage by the hour. It can be written into the parenting agreement that each parent is responsible for the electricity used while he or she is nesting. I must add though, I think the more room left in the parenting agreement for grace, the better.

* "Leaving the fridge empty and, worse yet, the condition of food left."

I understand that this can also be a cause of irritation for some people. My parenting agreement states that parents are responsible for feeding the children while they are nesting. I do more cooking then my ex, so I buy a lot more things that stay at the nest even when I'm not there. I don't mind if he uses the olive oil I purchased. For me it's a small price to pay.

* "Parents with different housekeeping standards—remember *The Odd Couple!*"

Again, I'm pretty laid back when it comes to housekeeping. My ex is neater when it comes to clutter and organization. But as long as his things are in order, he has the ability to look past the mess of others. That's one reason I choose to have a second master added to the nest. We can each live in our bedrooms and bathrooms the way we like. The common areas are another matter. We did not put anything in the parenting agreement specifically about cleaning the house, but we both leave it in what we think is good working order when we are handing it over to the other one. I will say that my ex has never mopped a floor in the nest. That's fine with me. It's basically the same as when we lived together. I do most of the cleaning. Again, I consider this a small sacrifice for the higher good of nesting.

* "Parents changing house rules for the children."

For me, this is one of the beauties of nesting. Each parent gets to parent the way he or she wants to. Isn't that what happens in a traditional custody situation anyway? Parents need to check their egos at the door. What if you think the kids need to go to bed at eight o'clock, and your ex thinks letting them stay up until nine is OK? If this is too much for you, if you wouldn't be able to sleep at night knowing your ex was letting your children watch PG-13 movies when you only allow G-rated movies, then you probably shouldn't nest. But remember, even if you don't, your ex can let the children watch whatever he or she wants. You have to let go of control.

* "Parents becoming resentful when friends are entertained by the other parent in their home."

Yes, this can be an issue if you let it. My ex and I both agreed that no unrelated people over the age of eighteen are allowed to stay overnight at the nest. This is written in our parenting agreement. As far as people visiting during the day, I trust my ex to put my children's best interests first. Any particular concerns can be addressed in the parenting agreement.

To Dr. Sommer's points, I would add the following:

* *What happens when someone gets married and maybe has more children?*

I see how this could be an issue. I'm fifty-three, and my ex-husband is sixty-two, so this probably isn't an issue for us. If one of us did remarry before our children left the nest, our parenting agreement would allow for that spouse to nest right along with the nesting parent. I don't know anyone who would want to sign up for that. If I did get married, I don't think I would want my new spouse to nest with me. It's too complicated.

For younger couples, the possibility of additional children is very real. If their family grew while they were nesting and the situation became too burdensome, then I suspect the co-parents would have to fall back to a more traditional custody arrangement. Things change.

* *Won't divorced parents be financially tied to each other if they have to maintain a nest together?*

Divorced parents are always financially tied to each other if they have children. Someone will be paying child support. In my parenting agreement, I am financially responsible for our nest. My ex-husband pays me child support. That's exactly what he would be doing if we weren't nesting. Raising children costs money no matter how the custody arrangement is written. There is no ethical way for a parent to get a "clean" break from a parenting commitment with their child's other parent unless there is some extreme circumstance.

The New Normal

● ● ●

Find the "narrow gate that leads to life." It is called
the Now. Narrow your life down to this moment.

ECKHART TOLLE

IT'S MEMORIAL DAY 2017. I'M sitting alone in my house, enjoy-
ing the filtered sunlight that shines brilliantly through the newly
installed sun tube in my living room at the farm. I've always felt
that there was more to sunlight than meets the eye. When I wake
up in the morning, if the sun is shining, I want that same illumina-
tion in my house.

My children are with their father at the nest today. I won-
der if they are doing anything special to acknowledge this holiday. Memorial Day will always be a marker for me now. It was
Memorial Day two years ago that the home I shared with my then
husband and my two children was destroyed by floodwaters. From
that destruction, we found a path to our much better, sunlit life.

Divorce is common in our culture, and it's just about accepted
as a normal part of life for a lot of people. Also accepted and almost
expected is that parenting after divorce will be complicated,

dysfunctional, and traumatic for the children and parents alike. It is also widely believed that as a result of divorce, children will have to be parented primarily by one parent or the other.

This has not been my experience. It is possible for both parents to equally parent the children after divorce in a way that is not complicated or traumatic. I have shared the intimate details of my experience with parenting after divorce so that others who are searching for ways to parent with their ex-spouses can see a real-life alternative to what is widely accepted as the best that can be done.

The nuclear family is still the best model for raising children. Nesting is a way to maintain the nuclear family even after divorce. Both parents are in the children's life equally, and the children are relieved of having to manage a hierarchy between their parents. My story is proof that divorce can be managed in a way to prevent broken homes. Love does conquer all. Relationships are evolving. Nesting will be a new normal for postdivorce parenting. Marriages end, but nesting can maintain continuity for the children of divorce. Nesting will be a new American institution.

● ● ●

TEXAS PARENTING AGREEMENT

PURSUANT TO TEXAS FAMILY CODE §153.0071, the parties to this agreement represent that this written parenting plan was reached at an informal settlement conference and is binding on the parties. The parties to this agreement, by their signatures below, agree that the terms of this agreement are just and right and are in the best interest of the children.

The parties agree that **THIS AGREEMENT IS BINDING AND IS NOT SUBJECT TO REVOCATION.**

███████████████ (mother) and ███████████████ (father), desiring individually and cooperatively to love and raise their mutual children, ███████████████ (daughter) and ███████ (son), within the context of a loving home and according to the values they hold in relation to spiritual and cultural matters, hereby enter into the following agreement. It is the mother and father's intention to share in the physical, emotional, and financial support of the children. The process that led to this agreement has been a considered and conscious one.

A. Nesting Agreement

1. Joint Custody. Father and mother shall have joint legal custody of their son and daughter. Joint custody means an arrangement by which parents share rights and responsibilities for major decisions concerning a child's residence, education, health care and religious training.

2. Nesting. Father and mother agree that they shall continue to share the family home ("nesting home") for the exercise of parenting time, an arrangement commonly referred to as "nesting." Both parents shall make arrangements for their own personal living accommodations outside of the family home for the periods during which they are not exercising their parenting time. For purposes of the parenting plan, a parent exercising his or her parenting time shall be designated the "Nesting Parent." The Nesting Parent shall have exclusive use of the nesting home. The other parent shall leave and shall not return to the nesting home, unless by invitation or prior approval of the Nesting Parent or due to an emergency or as otherwise set forth in this agreement.

3. Parenting Plan Schedule. Each parent's possession of the children is as follows:
   Two weeks at a time, alternating two-week periods of possession with the other parent, with one weeknight of possession exercised during each week of the period by the parent not otherwise in possession during that period, and subject to modification based on agreement by each parent. Each Parent shall have custody of the children for two weeks beginning and ending on Sunday evenings at 5:30 p.m.

B. Cooperation in Decision Making

1. Both parents will make decisions regarding health care, child care, and education by consensus. If a decision cannot be reached, both parents will utilize their procedures for resolving conflict set forth in section F below.
2. Consistency in child-rearing practices: Both parents agree that their child-rearing practices and everyday routines will be consistent with each other and will be discussed on an ongoing basis. These practices include, but are not limited to, diet, bedtime, television, and setting appropriate limits on the children's behavior.

C....
D. Financial Matters

1. Day-to-day expenses: The mother and father shall be individually responsible for food, clothing, toys, entertainment, and other day-to-day expenses incurred while they are residing in the common residence with the children.
2. Payment of common expenses: In order to facilitate the ease of maintaining the family home, the actual payment of common expense will be done by the mother. The father will pay $XXXXX per month to the mother in the form of child support on the first day of each month starting the month after this agreement signed.
3. Medical insurance: The children will have continuous medical insurance until they complete undergraduate studies or reach age twenty-five, whichever occurs sooner. The children will be covered by whichever parent's medical insurance offers the most comprehensive and least costly coverage for

the children. If the one parent obtains health insurance for the children through a place of employment, the other parent must reimburse the insuring parent 50 percent of the actual cost of insuring the children. Coverage may be provided for the children under both parents' medical insurance if such coverage is complimentary and no reimbursement is required.

4....

5. Life insurance: Both parents agree to provide funds for the care of the children in the event that one or both of the parents should die. The following life insurance policies that are in effect at the date of this order shall remain in effect until the younger child reaches twenty-two.

██████████ Life and Annuity
Policy Number: ██████████
Insured Name: ████████
Owner Name: ██████████
Policy Date: ████████
Product Name: Colony 20
Face Value: ████████
Beneficiary: ██████████

██████████ Life and Annuity
Policy Number: ██████████
Insured Name: ████████████
Owner Name: ██████████
Policy Date: ████████████
Product Name: Colony 20
Face Value: ████████
Beneficiary: ████████████

6. Income-tax benefits: Both parents will split income-tax benefits related to child-care expenses according to the actual financial contributions of each parent. Other tax deductions and credits will be taken by the parent who will accrue the largest financial benefit.

7. Disability insurance: Both parents will continue to maintain in effect a policy of disability insurance, or equivalent disability-insurance coverage, which is in effect at the time they sign this agreement.

8. Higher education: Both parents agree that it is their intention that the children receive a college education. Each parent agrees to contribute to the cost of this education. A college fund will be established with gifts and may be maintained by regular monthly or annual contributions by each parent. Both parents will confer annually to determine the amount of their contributions.

Each of us has read this agreement. Each of us understands and agrees to all of its terms.

_____   ███████████████

Mother's Name   Phone number

_____   _____

Mother's Signature   Date

_____   ███████████████

Father's Name   Phone number

_____   _____

Father's Signature   Date

STATE OF TEXAS

COUNTY OF _____

This instrument was acknowledged before me on _____ (date)
by _____
(name or names of person or persons acknowledging).

_____

Notary Public

Printed Name: _____

My Commission Expires:_____

REFERENCES

Flannery, Michael T. 2004. "Is Bird Nesting in the Best Interest of Children." *SMU Law Review* 57 (2): 295–352. http://scholar.smu.edu/smulr/vol57/iss2/2.

Kruk, Edward. 2013. "'Bird's Nest' Co-Parenting Arrangements." *Psychology Today* (blog), July 13. https://www.psychologytoday.com/blog/co-parenting-after-divorce/201307/birds-nest-co-parenting-arrangements.

"Sample Parenting Agreement between Mother and Father Who Are Both Biological Parents." n.d. MAIA Midwifery and Fertility. http://maiamidwifery.com/wp-content/uploads/2014/04/Parenting_Agreement_Mother_Father.pdf.

Sommer, Reena. 2012. "Nesting, an Option for Co-Parenting: A Good Idea in Principle but a Terrible One in Practise."*Custody Battle Counter Attack* (blog), August 20. http://blog.custodytrialconsultants.com/2012/08/nesting-for-co-parenting.html.

Notes about locations for your nest.

Notes about schools.

Notes about pets.

Notes about budgets.

Notes about supportive relatives.

Notes about supportive friends.

Notes about your children's friends.

Notes about your kid's activities.

Notes about special needs.

Notes about routines.

Notes about holidays.

Notes about college.

Notes about life insurance.

Notes about childcare.

Notes about housekeeping.

Notes about mediators.

Notes about lawyers.

Notes about your community.

Notes about your non-nesting living arrangements.

Notes about talking to your children.

Notes about how things will be better.

Notes about the atmosphere you want in the nest.

Notes of encouragement for yourself.

Notes of encouragement for your children.

Notes of encouragement for your ex.

Notes about.

Notes about.

Notes about.

Notes about.

Notes about.

Notes about.

Notes about.

Notes about.

Notes about.

Notes about.

Notes about.

Notes about.

Notes about.

Notes about.

Notes about.

Notes about.

Notes about.

Made in the USA
Monee, IL
27 May 2020

32049179R00079